NO LONGER PROPERTY OF THE
NORTH PROVIDENCE UNION FREE LIBRARY

North Providence Union Free Library
1810 Mineral Spring Avenue
North Providence, RI 02904
(401) 353-5600

GENDER IDENTITIES AND SEXUAL EXPRESSIONS

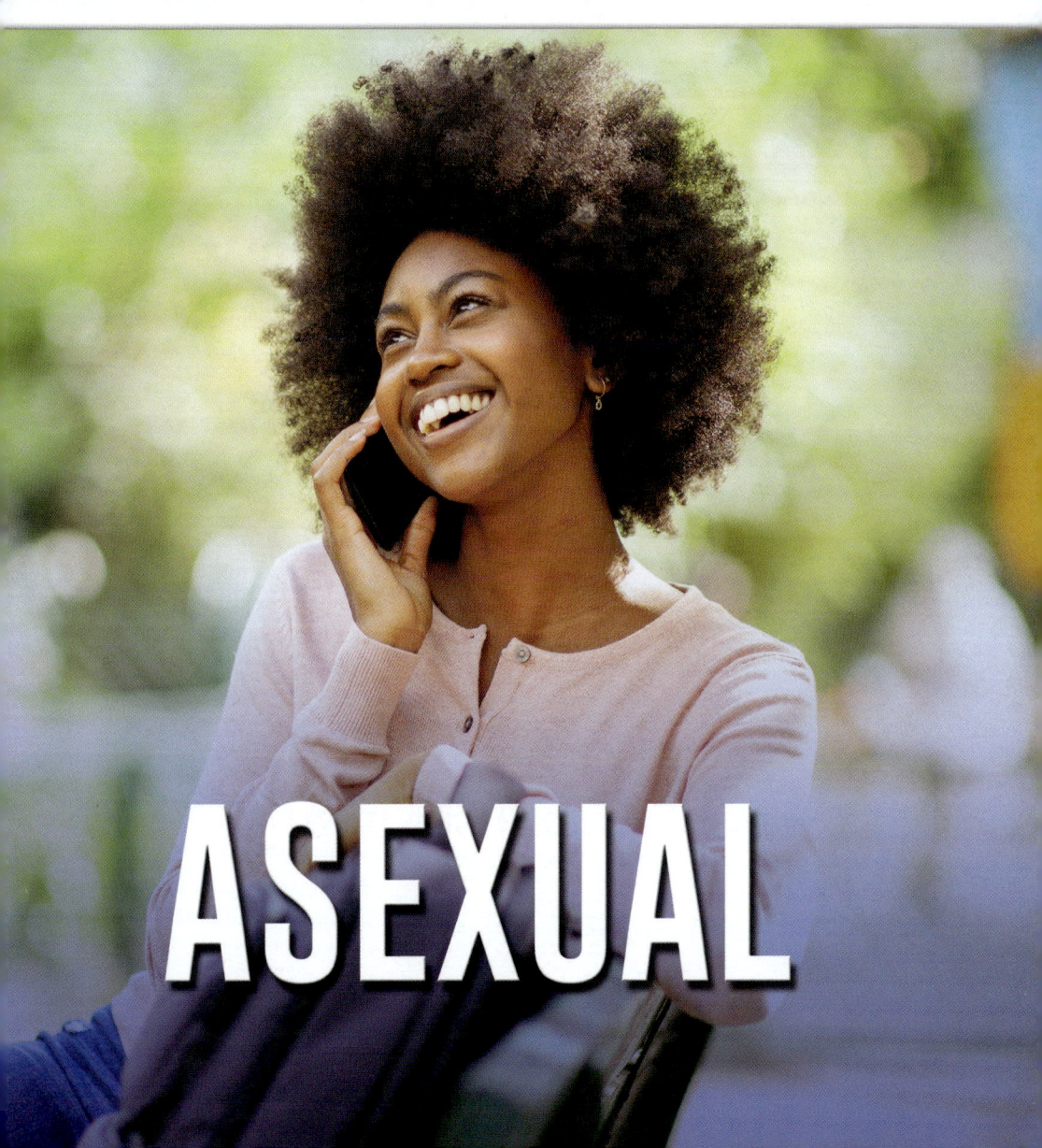

ASEXUAL

GENDER IDENTITIES AND SEXUAL EXPRESSIONS

ASEXUAL

BISEXUAL AND PANSEXUAL

FEMALE-TO-MALE TRANSGENDER AND TRANSMASCULINE IDENTITIES

GENDER EXPANSIVE

INTERSEX

MALE-TO-FEMALE TRANSGENDER AND TRANSFEMININE IDENTITIES

POLYAMOROUS

GENDER IDENTITIES AND SEXUAL EXPRESSIONS

ASEXUAL

By Jeremy Quist

MASON CREST
MIAMI

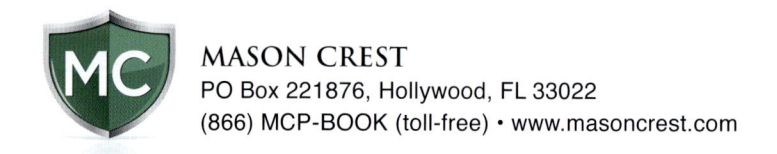

MASON CREST
PO Box 221876, Hollywood, FL 33022
(866) MCP-BOOK (toll-free) • www.masoncrest.com

Copyright © 2023 by Mason Crest, an imprint of National Highlights, Inc. All rights reserved. No part of this publication may be reproduced or transmitted in any form or by any means, electronic or mechanical, including photocopying, recording, taping, or any information storage and retrieval system, without permission in writing from the publisher.

Printed in the United States of America

First printing
9 8 7 6 5 4 3 2 1

Series ISBN: 978-1-4222-4694-8
Hardcover ISBN: 978-1-4222-4695-5
ebook ISBN: 978-1-4222-7117-9

Cataloging-in-Publication Data on file with the Library of Congress

Developed and Produced by Print Matters Productions, Inc
Cover and Interior Design by Torque Advertising+Design

Publisher's Note: Websites listed in this book were active at the time of publication. The publisher is not responsible for websites that have changed their address or discontinued operation since the date of publication. The publisher reviews and updates the websites each time the book is reprinted.

QR CODES AND LINKS TO THIRD-PARTY CONTENT

You may gain access to certain third-party content ("Third-Party Sites") by scanning and using the QR Codes that appear in this publication (the "QR Codes"). We do not operate or control in any respect any information, products, or services on such Third-Party Sites linked to by us via the QR Codes included in this publication, and we assume no responsibility for any materials you may access using the QR Codes. Your use of the QR Codes may be subject to terms, limitations, or restrictions set forth in the applicable terms of use or otherwise established by the owners of the Third-Party Sites. Our linking to such Third-Party Sites via the QR Codes does not imply an endorsement or sponsorship of such Third-Party Sites or the information, products, or services offered on or through the Third-Party Sites, nor does it imply an endorsement or sponsorship of this publication by the owners of such Third-Party Sites.

CONTENTS

Introduction: Gender Identity and Sexual Expression .. 6
Chapter 1: What Does It Mean to Be Asexual? 12
Chapter 2: Figuring Out You: A Work in Progress...... 28
Chapter 3: The Life: Language, Culture, Law, and Community 44
Chapter 4: Taking Care of Yourself: Health and Medicine 60
Chapter 5: Coming Out: A Personal Decision............ 74
Series Glossary of Key Terms 88
Further Reading & Internet Resources 92
Index.. 94
Author's Biography and Credits 96

KEY ICONS TO LOOK FOR:

Words to Understand: These words with their easy-to-understand definitions will increase the reader's understanding of the text while building vocabulary skills.

Sidebars: This boxed material within the main text allows readers to build knowledge, gain insights, explore possibilities, and broaden their perspectives by weaving together additional information to provide realistic and holistic perspectives.

Educational Videos: Readers can view videos by scanning our QR codes, providing them with additional educational content to supplement the text. Examples include news coverage, moments in history, speeches, iconic sports moments, and much more!

Text-Dependent Questions: These questions send the reader back to the text for more careful attention to the evidence presented there.

Research Projects: Readers are pointed toward areas of further inquiry connected to each chapter. Suggestions are provided for projects that encourage deeper research and analysis.

Series Glossary of Key Terms: This back-of-the-book glossary contains terminology used throughout this series. Words found here increase the reader's ability to read and comprehend higher-level books and articles in this field.

INTRODUCTION

GENDER IDENTITY AND SEXUAL EXPRESSION

Infinite diversity in infinite combinations.
—Gene Roddenberry, creator of *Star Trek*

We don't have to tell you how crazy and overwhelming life can be when you are near or in your teenage years. You're bombarded with ideas from all sorts of sources—including your own mind. You may find that you're feeling all the things the YA novels and sex ed classes say you're supposed to feel. Or you may feel that your experience doesn't look anything like what you see around you.

That's why we created this series about gender identity and sexual orientation. People with experiences, feelings, and identities that don't fall into the so-called normal boxes are in need of information. And even if you happen to be both hetero and cisgendered, it's almost certain that there are people you care about who are not.

These books can provide answers to some basic questions, as well as helping you define a direction for your inquiries going forward. You may also find things in these books that you don't agree with. That's okay. The truth is, gender and sexuality are highly individual, and no one person's experience is going to look exactly like another's. Also, there's a good chance that, just as older textbooks on sexuality have become outdated, ideas about LGBTQIA folks are going to evolve beyond what we're writing here today.

As a species, we are still figuring it out. Our understanding of sex, gender, attraction, and relationships is still in its infancy.

Gender and sexuality are highly individual. No person's experience is going to look exactly like another's.

It wasn't long ago that we were limited to visual examinations to determine a baby's sex at birth—one of two boxes had to be checked. In some cases, the choice of a blue or pink ribbon on a hospital bassinet came down to a guess. Now, with access to more genetic information, we are understanding that many people who were presumed to be cisgendered are in fact intersex. Neuroscience is catching up as well, confirming that a person's brain has as much to do with their gender as their chromosomes do—something trans folk have always known.

It is not just possible, but likely, that many ideas commonly held today about gender, sexuality, and relationships will eventually be found to be either simplistic or incorrect. As individuals, we need to explore for ourselves to better understand our identities, what kinds of people we are attracted to, and what sorts of romantic relationships we desire.

Introduction: Gender Identity and Sexual Expression

We are who we are. That deserves space, acceptance, and respect.

In the Gender Identities and Sexual Expressions series, we'll provide a primer and a basic roadmap for navigating different aspects of gender and sexuality. These include:

- gender identity
- sexual attraction
- relationship structures that include polyamory

It's okay to be unsure or to have questions about who you are and who you are attracted to. Many people find that their attractions vary as they travel through different environments and as they live through different phases of their lives. That doesn't mean that what you feel about who you are and what you want is "just a phase." It means that humans are complex, multifaceted, and unlikely to fit neatly into any particular box.

In addition to helping you understand the diversity of identities and orientations, our goal is to give you the tools to safely navigate a wide range of situations. We'll discuss sexual health, emotional and mental well-being, legal protections, and issues like coping with prejudice.

Increasingly Visible Identities and Orientations

Early in 2021, a Gallup poll produced results that few members of Generation Z (Gen Zs) would find surprising: a larger number of Americans identified as LGBTQIA than ever before. In total, 5.6 percent of the adult population identified as gay, lesbian, bisexual, trans, or questioning (compared with 3.5 percent in the polling company's first such survey in 2012).

Among Americans who said they were LGBTQIA, a little more than half identified as bisexual. An additional 36.2 percent of those who identified as LGBTQIA described themselves as gay or lesbian. Just over 11 percent of the LGBTQIA respondents identified themselves as transgender. A separate set of surveys conducted by the Williams Institute indicated that there are around one million people in the United States who identify as nonbinary.

The younger the respondent, the more likely they were to identify as something other than cisgender and straight. While only about 2 percent of baby boomers said they were LGBTQIA, 16 percent of people, or nearly one in six, between the ages of 18 and 23 did.

We're not in a place to comment with any certainty on why this is true. Some people think that previous generations were more afraid of backlash, and thus were more likely to stay closeted and hide these parts of their identities. Others theorize that a lack of open discussion and information meant that many people never had a chance to fully explore their own identities and attractions. Chances are that both of these are factors.

But, in the end, the *why* doesn't matter. We are who we are. That deserves space, acceptance, and respect.

Gender and Sexuality Are Separate

One thing to establish at the outset: gender and sexual attraction are separate. Gender is who you are, whether you feel you are a man, a woman, something in between, or neither one. Sexual attraction refers to who you are attracted to.

These exist on entirely separate axes and are completely independent from one another. You can be FTM (female to male) transgender, and be attracted to men, women, both, or neither. A butch-presenting cis woman may be a lesbian, or she may be gender noncomforming and hetero. There are no rules that dictate who someone should be attracted to.

Changing Ideas about Relationships

In 2015, the Supreme Court of the United States recognized a right several states had already enshrined: the right to marry

Gender and sexual attraction are separate. Regardless of gender identity, there are no rules that dictate who someone should be attracted to.

someone of the same sex. Even a couple of decades earlier, this was seen as an impossible goal. Now you see married, same-sex couples on HGTV.

Polyamory, or relationships that involve more than two people, has always been around. While it was blatantly outlawed in some states and countries, this has always been a way that some people have chosen to love. There is more open conversation of polyamorous relationships today than ever before. Some people find that this is an arrangement that they want in every romantic relationship. Sometimes, it is what they want in a specific time of their life, or with specific people.

There are also gradients when it comes to levels of attraction. Someone who is asexual may be gay, straight, or something else. They may be romantically attracted to people even if they don't experience attraction sexually.

This Is Your Journey, Take It at Your Own Pace

It's not even a little uncommon to lack a strong definition of who you are and what you want. This is true at any age. Bisexual people in hetero relationships may wonder if they're bisexual enough. Someone who is asexual may question whether this is just how they feel right now, or if this is baked into who they are, and will continue to be how they feel for life. Yet another person may find that they can't quite put a finger on why they don't always feel at home in the gender they were assigned at birth.

All of this is valid. It's equally valid and normal to have a defined and unshakeable understanding of your sexuality, your gender, and what sorts of relationships you think that you will want.

After all, the world is an infinitely varied place, full of unique wonders.

You're one of them.

There is a growing awareness that sexuality is not as simple as was once thought.

WORDS TO UNDERSTAND

Aromantic: Referring to a sexual orientation in which a person is not interested in forming a romantic relationship.

Asexual: Referring to a sexual orientation in which a person is not sexually attracted to anyone.

Demisexual: Referring to a sexual orientation in which a person is only sexually attracted to someone after forming a deep emotional bond.

Gray-asexual: Referring to a sexual orientation in which a person feels a very limited sexual attraction, often only within very specific circumstances.

Sexual orientation: An identity that expresses whom someone is sexually attracted to.

CHAPTER 1

WHAT DOES IT MEAN TO BE ASEXUAL?

"I realized I was **asexual** around the same time my peers seemed to realize that they were not," the model Yasmin Benoit wrote in *Teen Vogue*. "Once the hormones kicked in, so did a nearly universal interest in sex for those around me. . . . I had no sexual desire towards other people, I did not experience sexual attraction, and that hasn't changed."

One of Many Sexual Orientations

Most of the time, when people discuss **sexual orientation**, they mention three options: heterosexual, homosexual, and bisexual. There is a growing awareness that sexuality is not that simple and that many other options exist along a spectrum. But even this more complex, nuanced way of framing things can exclude a wide range of other sexualities.

A person on one far end of the spectrum is attracted solely to people who are of their own gender and feel no attraction to the other; a person on the far other end of the spectrum is attracted solely to people of the opposite gender and feels

One definition of asexuality is the total lack of sexual attraction to anyone.

nothing for their own. Most people experience some sort of more complex combination of the two. Pansexuality takes into consideration the wide range of other gender identities beyond just male or female. Asexuality, meanwhile, lies entirely outside of this spectrum.

How Asexuality Is Different

One strict definition of *asexuality* would be the total lack of sexual attraction to anyone. Since a sexual orientation describes whom a person is attracted to sexually, asexuality is just as valid a sexual orientation as any other.

For an asexual person, society's seeming obsession with sex is completely baffling. They hear their friends talk about people of the gender or genders they are attracted to in rapturous words, barely able to contain their desire for these people. They see advertising using attraction to get people interested in their products. ("Sex sells," as they say.) They hear songs about how much someone wants to take someone else to bed.

You Want to Do *What*?

None of what an asexual person observes in others seems to reflect their own experience. They don't see someone on the street and find their mind wandering into erotic territory. Seeing a person with few clothes on does not make them want to purchase something from a company. And though they may be able to appreciate a good beat, no music is to going to make them want to grind up against someone.

This apparent difference in how they experience the world can create a feeling of isolation or distance from their peers. They may feel the need to fake attractions in order to fit in. They may feel pressured into situations that don't really appeal to them. Others may be unable to understand asexuals and make them feel weird for their perfectly natural inclination.

As with other sexual and gender minorities, when "aces" (as asexuals often refer to themselves) find that there is a word that describes how they feel and that there are others in the same situation, it can be an eye-opening and affirming experience. If you find that what you read about in this book describes your thoughts and feelings, know that those thoughts and feelings are just as valid as everyone else's. And you are not alone in how you feel.

The Asexuality Umbrella

Just as the concepts of heterosexual, homosexual, and bisexual are overly simplistic, a strict definition of asexuality can be limiting as well. Many people find themselves relating to the idea of asexuality, but with an asterisk. These people *generally*

David Jay, founder of the Asexual Visibility and Education Network (AVEN), explains the need to acknowledge asexuality.

do not feel sexual attraction toward others, but under certain circumstances they might.

People with these feelings are considered to be under the "asexuality umbrella" or on the "ace spectrum" Various terms have been created to help people more accurately and precisely describe how they feel, which we're going to discuss.

There is sometimes confusion as to how people who do occasionally feel sexual attraction can be considered asexual, or at least can be under the asexuality umbrella. The one thing that they all have in common is feeling outside the dominant culture's preoccupation with sex. They can't relate to the attitudes toward sex and sexual attraction held by most others (people who are not part of under the asexual umbrella).

Gray-Asexual

Sexuality is not always black and white. Many people find themselves in gray areas, not in one thing or the other. The term **gray-asexual** recognizes this complexity. These are the people who feel the need for an asterisk on their asexuality—meaning "further explanation required."

Sometimes people consider themselves asexual, and then one day they are surprised by a sexual attraction that they didn't expect to feel. It doesn't mean that they are suddenly unwelcome in the asexual community. They don't lose their membership card. They have just found that their sexuality is more complex than they had previously thought.

Another person may just feel a very low-level attraction—maybe so low that they find the idea of having sex unappealing. Maybe a situation has to fit a very specific set of circumstances in order to produce attraction—specific enough that it rarely happens.

Someone like this may choose to identify as gray-asexual, also sometimes referred to as "gray-sexual" or "gray-A."

For demisexuals, sexual attraction does not exist until after a deep connection.

Demisexual

There are different ways in which the "gray" in gray-asexual manifests itself. Some of those ways are described above. For a **demisexual**, that gray comes only after they have formed a deep emotional connection to someone, which can come in many different forms. It can start as a platonic friendship and evolve into something else. It can be a dating situation that begins without real sexual attraction, and then over time (usually an extended period) an emotional bond forms, followed by a sexual attraction.

    Just choosing not to have sex with a significant other until after a deep emotional connection has formed is not the same as being a demisexual. Most dating relationships contain a

FIGURING OUT HER DEMISEXUALITY

A young woman named Genevieve shared her experience of finding a relationship as a demisexual with *Wired* magazine: "She met James online. After months of close friendship, they dated for a year long-distance, and then she moved to Tennessee to be nearer to him. 'I knew we didn't line up in terms of sex drive, but he didn't hold it against me,' she says. He was patient—very patient. It would be three years after they met that she felt the pull of desire for the first time and their relationship became sexual. 'I think when I knew him so well that when my heart decided he was my soul mate, my body decided so too.'"

sexual attraction; people may just choose not to act on it. For demisexuals, the attraction itself does not exist until after the deep connection has been established.

Asexuality and Relationships

One common misconception about asexuality is that aces, by definition, do not have romantic relationships. That is simply not the case. Many aces feel a desire for other types of connections than the physical. Many choose to have relationships—even marriages.

Love and sex are not inseparable. Many sexual people can understand the concept of sex without love in the form of casual sex and one-night stands. But they might have a harder time understanding love without sex. For aces, however, this makes just as much sense (or even more sense).

*Many asexual people choose to have relationships—
even marriages.*

When discussing sexual orientations such as heterosexual, homosexual, bisexual, and pansexual, it's generally assumed that we are designating both whom a person is sexually attracted to and whom they are interested in having a romantic relationship with. With aces, these concepts are complicated because the sexual attraction part of that formula is removed. So how do we talk about someone who is asexual but interested in a romantic relationship?

Romantic Orientation

To communicate a person's feelings toward relationships, it's common for people in the asexual community to identify with a romantic orientation. Just as a sexual orientation communicates whom you're interested in having a sexual relationship with, a romantic orientation communicates whom you're interested in having a romantic relationship with.

If a person identifies as asexual but feels an interest in having an emotional relationship with someone of the same sex, they might describe themselves as being "asexual homoromantic." Similarly, other people can use terms we associate with sexual orientation to describe their romantic orientation. A person can identify as asexual heteroromantic, biromantic, or panromantic (orientation that is not linked to a person's gender).

Just as a person can be asexual, they can also be **aromantic**, meaning they don't have any interest in forming a romantic relationship. If someone wants to communicate that they are only interested in a relationship after a deep connection, they can also describe themselves as "demiromantic."

Similar terms exist for others within the asexuality umbrella. A person can identify as demisexual homoromantic, gray-asexual panromantic, asexual aromantic, or any other combination of these identities.

Just as a person can be asexual, they can also be aromantic.

What Asexuality Is Not

People sometimes confuse celibacy and abstinence with asexuality, so it's useful to define these words to point out the differences. Abstinence implies a conscious choice to not have sex. This decision could be made for religious or moral reasons, a desire to wait for a particular set of circumstances, or plenty of other possible reasons. But abstinence still usually implies a desire to have sex, combined with a conscious decision to not act on it. Asexuality is the lack of a desire to do so.

Celibacy is similar, but it implies a long-term commitment. The word is most commonly used to describe a religious vow someone has taken to abstain from sexual contact, such as a priest or another religious figure.

Neither of these definitions precludes a sexual attraction. Asexuality is a sexual orientation—a statement of whom someone is attracted to (in this case, no one). Abstinence and celibacy describe a person's behavior. Aces may be abstinent or celibate, but that is separate from their asexuality.

When an Ace Might Have a Physical Relationship

As stated above, since asexuality is a sexual orientation, the word describes feelings, not behavior. A lack of sexual desire does not mean that someone is incapable of having sex. This might seem counterintuitive to some. How can an asexual person have sex? The short answer is that typically an ace's body parts are just as functional as anyone else's. The long answer will be discussed more in Chapter 4.

So why would an ace have some sort of sexual contact with someone? There are myriad reasons. They might be curious about what all the fuss is about. They may have a significant other who is sexual, and want to make that person happy. While no one should ever be pressured into having sex, sometimes mixed-orientation couples find some compromise to be necessary. For gray-asexuals, it may just be a matter of their prerequisites being met.

Sex may still be pleasurable for an ace. Aces don't find physical intimacy necessary in the way that sexual people do, but often the body's physical responses are the same. Some aces describe sex as somewhat pleasurable; they'd just rather be playing a video game, eating cake, or doing just about anything else they enjoy.

Attitudes toward Sex

This leads us to another common misconception about asexuality. Aces are not necessarily anti-sex. It doesn't mean

Aces are not necessarily anti-sex.

that they are disgusted by sex and everyone who participates in sexual activity.

Within the ace umbrella, there is a wide range of attitudes toward sex. Some may find it truly repellent. Others don't really have a problem with it, but they just don't feel the need for it. Some may be able to compromise with a partner in order to occasionally have sexual intimacy for their benefit. Others are just completely incapable of doing so.

These attitudes can be divided into three categories: sex-favorable, sex-indifferent, and sex-averse/sex-repulsed. "sex-favorable," according to asexuality.org, means "a positive willingness to compromise with a sexual partner, openness to finding ways to enjoy sexual activity in a physical or emotional

There is no right or wrong way to be asexual/gray-sexual/demisexual.

way, happy to give sexual pleasure rather than receive." "Sex-Indifferent" means that they are less likely to compromise to a significant degree but aren't disgusted by the thought. And "sex-averse/sex-repulsed" refers to "a distressed or visceral reaction to the thought of having sex."

Tying It All Together

There is no right or wrong way to be asexual/gray-sexual/demisexual. The one thing that ties it all together is a general lack of sexual attraction in most situations. Everything else is a matter of shades and degrees.

As Isabel Corp, a college student at the New School in New York City, told GLAAD, "There are misconceptions that asexuals are just late bloomers, that we've never experienced sexual or romantic attraction before, or our experiences all look the same, which couldn't be further from the truth. Asexuality is a spectrum, and many of us experience attraction (or lack thereof) in different ways."

TEXT-DEPENDENT QUESTIONS

1. What is asexuality? How is it different from other sexual orientations?
2. How is asexuality different from abstinence and celibacy?
3. What is demisexuality, and how does it vary from other sexual orientations?

RESEARCH PROJECTS

1. Use HuffPost's article on "The Asexual Spectrum" (https://www.huffpost.com/entry/asexual-spectrum_n_3428710) to research the various identities within the asexual spectrum. Draw a chart of your own, however you like, to visually represent how they relate to each other.
2. Now add to your chart the various romantic orientations and how they relate to each other. Connect sexual orientations and romantic orientations to each other with lines, and use them to describe how the combinations might identify.

Sexuality and identity are incredibly complicated issues.

WORDS TO UNDERSTAND

Acearo: A person who identifies as both asexual (ace) and aromantic (aro).

Aesthetic attraction: A nonsexual appreciation of a person's appearance.

Allosexual: Someone who feels sexual attraction to other people.

Aspec: Another way to refer to the asexual spectrum and those on it.

Libido: A body's urges, usually associated with a person's sex drive.

Queerplatonic: A relationship that goes beyond just friendship but never becomes sexual or romantic.

CHAPTER 2

FIGURING OUT YOU: A WORK IN PROGRESS

"I always just assumed I would want it eventually when the time was right," 21-year-old Kayla told *Cosmopolitan*. "But I reflected and realized that the time may never be right. In my last relationship, I was very much in love, and we were together for almost two and a half years. Still, the time was never right.

"Then, I remembered that I heard the term *asexual* come up back when I was in high school. I decided to look it up. I researched for hours and hours and hours that day . . . Everything just sort of clicked."

Patience with the Process

Sexuality and identity are incredibly complicated issues. For many people, it's a lifelong journey to understand themselves, who they are, and what makes them happy. There's no deadline for when you *ought to* have it all figured out. Adolescence is a perfect time to explore which labels, if any, help us describe ourselves to the world, but there is absolutely not a timer that counts down to when we must have an answer.

Labels are only tools to help us. They can help us communicate who we are to those we care about. They can help us find community with those who feel similarly. They can help us tell a potential romantic partner what they can expect from us in a relationship.

If you find labels making your life more difficult instead of easier, it's okay to not settle on one. It's okay to not identify as any term that other people have created to describe themselves.

But it also may be that one of these labels speaks to you and your feelings.

Am I Asexual?

I've never had a relationship, **or** *I've never had a good relationship—maybe I'm just asexual.*

I've never had sex. I've never even made it to second base (whatever that even means)—maybe I'm just asexual.

Sometimes dating just doesn't seem worth it—maybe I'm just asexual.

It's important to remember that asexuality is a sexual orientation and therefore refers to a person's feelings of attraction. It has nothing to do with a person's relationship history or sexual history. Those can be indications, but they're by no means automatically tied together.

Asexuality is a general lack of sexual interest. If you find yourself desiring some type of sexual interaction with another person on a regular basis, that's not asexuality. Aces feel no loss in not having the degree of sexual interaction that others seem to expect. They don't long for it or fantasize about it. Their brains just don't work that way.

Asexuality has nothing to do with a person's relationship history or sexual history.

Chapter 2: Figuring Out You: A Work in Progress

Listen to asexual people explain what the word means to them.

Asexual Crushes

I find myself forming crushes on people. I think about them a lot and think about how much I like being around them—I must not be asexual.

Asexual people describe their romantic orientation in addition to their sexual orientation. It's very common for aces to want a romantic relationship or other types of deep emotional connection. Wanting to hold hands, cuddle in front of the TV, or enjoy the company of one particular person day in and day out is not inherently sexual.

Aces also sometimes describe an **aesthetic attraction**, meaning that they can appreciate the looks (or aesthetics) of a person without a sexual component. It's closer to how someone

For an asexual person, sexual physical reactions are not necessarily directed toward a particular person.

would recognize the beauty of a piece of art or beauty in nature. They recognize that someone is objectively pleasant to look at without feeling a sexual attraction.

Arousal

I sometimes feel aroused. I even masturbate sometimes—I must not be asexual.

    Not necessarily. Aces may still find their bodies wanting stimulation, and they often have the same physical reactions to that stimulation as anyone else.

    The difference is that for an asexual it's not directed toward someone. They don't see a particular person and become aroused. Some asexual people masturbate. For **allosexuals** (people outside the ace spectrum), that can be confusing, because for them, masturbation is often tied to sexual fantasies. Aces may have an emotional or romantic crush, but they don't fantasize about sexual contact with that crush, so that type of fantasy is not part of masturbation for them. It's purely a physical response.

Libido

A person's **libido** is a separate, though related, issue from their sexuality. *Libido* refers more to the urges or needs of a person's body and has less to do with emotion or attraction. According to a 2017 research study by Ritch Savin-Williams, asexuals are less likely to masturbate on a regular basis, but a majority still do. The study concluded that asexual women and men who masturbated did so because they felt they "had to," not because it was particularly sexually pleasurable or fun. The focus is on physical sensations rather than erotic images; that is, their masturbation is more motivated by physical needs ("akin to an itch needing to be scratched") than by innate sexual desire or arousal.

Masturbation is also different for aces in that their fantasies are less likely to be about having sex with another person. Their focus is more likely to be on their own body or sexual situations between other people, not including themselves.

Am I Gray-Asexual?

I relate to the idea of asexuality, but the description doesn't fit me perfectly—I guess that means I'm not asexual.

Within the asexual spectrum, sometimes referred to as **aspec**, there is a wide range of diversity in people's experience with occasional sexual attraction. People who feel some attraction, but still generally relate to asexuality, will often identify as gray-asexual.

Asexual

An ace's fantasies are less likely to be about having sex with another person.

Chapter 2: Figuring Out You: A Work in Progress 35

The definition of gray-asexuality is very broad and is a constant subject of conversation within the ace community. But the community is generally inclusive and doesn't expect people to satisfy a list of requirements in order to use the labels they have created.

Am I Demisexual?

I think I might be asexual, but I have a friend I have become very close to and sometimes feel a sexual attraction to—I must not be asexual.

This is a common experience for many people within the gray-asexual community. For these gray-aces, an attraction is based on emotional traits. An appreciation of physical appearance may come later, but an emotional attraction comes first. The amount of time it takes to get to that point varies. It could be days, months, or years, depending on the person.

A person who only experiences attraction after a very deep emotional connection has formed may choose to identify as a demisexual, which is a subset of gray-asexuality.

Demisexuality as Sexual Orientation

I want to wait to have sex until I'm in a serious relationship/married. I find the idea of having sex with someone I don't know really, well, scary and/or uncomfortable—I must be demisexual.

Not necessarily. There are plenty of valid reasons to not rush into a sexual relationship; a person being demisexual is just one of those. No matter your sexual orientation, no one should be pressuring you into sexual activity. If a person doesn't feel ready for any reason, that's perfectly valid, independent of their sexual orientation.

That doesn't automatically mean that they are part of the ace umbrella. Demisexuality describes whom a person is attracted to, not what they choose to do with that attraction. If

There are plenty of valid reasons to not rush into a sexual relationship.

a person feels attractions to people on a regular basis but just doesn't like the idea of acting on that attraction without other conditions being met, that's not what would usually be referred to as demisexuality.

Queerplatonic Relationships

I can relate to demisexuality in that I form very strong relationships, but they don't really become either sexual or romantic.

The ace community has come up with the concept of a **queerplatonic** relationship. This is the idea that relationships can exist that are beyond what we would normally consider friendship but do not become sexual or romantic.

Listen to demisexual people explain what the word means to them.

Our language is so often limited in so many areas. Of course, most of us would know that this type of relationships exists, but there is such an emphasis in our culture on sexuality and romantic love that we never have even bothered coming up with a word for it until lately.

Combining Identities

We've already discussed how a romantic orientation can interact with an asexual, gray-sexual, or demisexual orientation. But other sexual orientations can also have some overlap with the ace umbrella of orientations. For example, if a person mostly identifies with asexuality, gray-sexuality, or demisexuality but does occasionally feel sexual attraction, they may feel that limited sexual attraction toward a certain gender or genders. They can combine gray-bisexual, demi-heterosexual, and other combinations. Then, combined with romantic orientation, we may see, as just one example, people identifying as heteroromantic gray-bisexual, which would mean that a person feels an occasional sexual attraction to people of either gender but feels a stronger romantic pull toward people of the opposite gender.

Another example could be a person who identifies as aromantic gray-pansexual, which would mean that they could be attracted to anyone of any gender on occasion but are uninterested in having a romantic relationship.

Sometimes these identity combinations come up with their own lingo and way of talking about themselves. For example, "asexual aromantic" is sometimes shortened to **acearo**.

WHERE DO THE WORDS COME FROM?

Though the word *asexual* **has been around in English for a long time, some of the other terms used by the asexual community are pretty new. Many of them originated in the online forum of AVEN, the Asexual Visibility and Education Network.**

The idea of gray-asexuality/gray-ace evolved on AVEN as some people realized that their asexuality was not quite as complete as others' was. The word *demisexuality* **originated on the AVEN boards in 2006. It comes from the Latin word** *dimidium***, which means something that is divided in half. The idea is that demisexuality splits the spectrum between sexual and asexual in half.**

Chapter 2: Figuring Out You: A Work in Progress

Evolving Identity

The ace community is very open to the idea of people evolving in how they refer to themselves as they explore their sexuality. It's okay for a person to identify as asexual and then realize that maybe they're more of a demisexual. It's equally alright for a demisexual to find that maybe they're grayer than they thought.

The same is true of romantic orientations. Maybe someone thinks that they are aromantic but then decides that they want to try a relationship. It's okay to change your identity from aromantic to gray-romantic, biromantic, heteroromantic, homoromantic, or panromantic. And if, after trying, that person decides that they were right in the first place and really has no interest in a romantic relationship, they can then identify again as aromantic.

Sexual Orientation and Gender Identity

A person's sexual orientation, whether ace, straight, gay, bi, pan, or anything else, is completely separate from their gender identity. Gender identity refers to whether a person feels themselves to be male, female, agender, genderqueer, or one of a number of other options. Like the other identities we are discussing in this book, gender lies on a spectrum.

An *agender* person is one who doesn't identify with either male or female. *Genderqueer* refers to a person who feels like they combine gender identities in a way that makes them neither male nor female; in other words, somewhere on the spectrum between the two.

Though a person's sexual orientation can be informed by their gender and/or the gender of those they are attracted to (to whatever degree that might be), sexual orientation and gender identity are separate issues.

A person's sexual orientation is completely separate from their gender identity.

Chapter 2: Figuring Out You: A Work in Progress

Your Identity, Your Choice

At the end of the day, the words you use to describe yourself to others are completely your choice to make. No one else can tell you what you are or aren't.

Most of the terms we've discussed here are relatively new. Of course, there have always been people who have felt these ways; it's just that people are finding new ways of communicating their feelings and new ways of finding community based upon their identity.

With that in mind, it's important to remember that these ideas are still evolving as people refine how they communicate what is going on inside of them. You may find these words being used in slightly different ways in different contexts.

Terms and labels are tools to be used if they are useful to you in your situation. With all of these ideas combined, including sexual orientation, romantic orientation, and gender identity, it's possible to give others a pretty detailed idea of who we are in a way that was not possible before the terms were created.

TEXT-DEPENDENT QUESTIONS

1. If a person feels a low level of sexual attraction but relates more to asexuality, do they have to identify as allosexual? How might they identify?
2. How might someone who has attraction to any gender after forming a strong relationship, but who only sees themselves having a relationship with someone of their own gender, describe themselves?
3. What is a queerplatonic relationship?

RESEARCH PROJECT

Find an article online that shows someone sharing their experience of realizing that they are somewhere on the ace spectrum. Summarize the person's story. What was their process of discovery?

The idea of "ace" as an identity really came into the culture through the Internet.

WORDS TO UNDERSTAND

AVEN: Asexuality Visibility and Education Network.

LGBTQ: An acronym standing for "lesbian, gay, bisexual, transgender, and queer"; asexual could be considered part of "queer."

LGBTQIA+: A more inclusive acronym that includes "intersex" and "asexual" explicitly.

Queer: A blanket term used to describe all of those who exist outside of the cisgender heterosexual experience.

CHAPTER 3

THE LIFE: LANGUAGE, CULTURE, LAW, AND COMMUNITY

"My favorite part of being asexual is the community," says Addie Orr, a student at the University of Alabama, while speaking with GLAAD. "Asexual people tend to get each other in a way that is incredibly unique and incredibly rewarding. I remember the first time I learned about asexuality, I immediately started crying. Other people thought like me. I wasn't weird or wrong. And when I came out, I was immediately surrounded by fellow asexuals that continue to validate me and give me support."

A Community for the Asexual Spectrum

Though asexuality has always existed, the idea of "ace" as an identity really came into the culture through the Internet. It was the ability of those on the ace spectrum to find each other online and realize that there were many others who felt the same way that they did that allowed for the creation of the many terms and identities within the umbrella.

In 2001, a college student named David Jay realized that there was a need for community for those like him. As a result,

DISCUSS

CLICK HERE TO CHAT

It didn't take long for AVEN to become the prominent aspec community forum.

Asexual

he founded the **Asexuality Visibility and Education Network (AVEN)** to help asexuals find each other. Jay has been a prominent advocate for the ace community ever since, appearing many times in the media raising cultural awareness of the existence of an asexual identity.

AVEN

It didn't take long for AVEN to become the most prominent aspec community forum, allowing tens of thousands of people to come to understand themselves better and to find others who feel the same way. The AVEN discussion boards are where many of the ways that we describe the modern ace experience were first used. Terms that we've already discussed, like *gray-sexual* and *demisexual*, had their start there.

Generally, the AVEN discussion boards are welcoming places for those who are trying to figure themselves out. The AVEN forum community guidelines spell it out: "Making judgments about other users, especially about the validity of their asexuality, is strongly discouraged. We are here to figure ourselves out, not to put each other in boxes."

For those questioning whether they fit on the asexual spectrum, the AVEN website (asexuality.org) can be an invaluable resource. For many, it is the first stop on their journey of self-discovery.

The Signs of Community

Every community has its own signs and symbols, things that signal to those in-the-know that you are one of them. As the ace community is still a young one, these parts of the subculture are still being developed. Despite its youth, though, some hallmarks of the culture have already become very popular in ace groups and websites.

In 2017, two friends started a podcast called Sounds Fake But Okay.

A PODCAST FOR ACES

In 2017, two friends started a podcast called *Sounds Fake But Okay*. Sarah Costello is asexual aromantic (acearo), and Kayla Kaszyca is demisexual and straight. On their podcast, they talk "about all things to do with love, relationships, sexuality, and pretty much anything else that they just don't understand."

Sounds Fake But Okay has become one of the most popular, most visible pieces of aspec pop culture.

These signs can be large and small, serious or funny. The ace community has its in-jokes and code words, like every other subculture. As the Asexuality Archive forewarns, "At some point, you may notice that some groups of asexuals seem to have a strange obsession with cake. This isn't because asexuals are all secretly bakers. Rather, it's because cake is clearly better than sex, something that asexuals and non-asexuals can agree on."

A Flag to Represent

Ever since the adoption of the rainbow flag as a symbol of **LGBTQ** pride, it's common for sexual and gender minorities to create their own flags to represent themselves. After extensive discussions on online ace forums, a design was settled on for a flag that has been used ever since.

The asexual flag can be seen more and more often at LGBTQ events.

Where Asexuality Fits within the LGBTQ Community

There has been some confusion over the years within the LGBTQ community about what asexuality is and where it fits as a sexual orientation among the others. Awareness is increasing, however, and more and more LGBTQ organizations are becoming explicitly inclusive. In addition, it's becoming more and more common to see aspecs represented at LGBTQ Pride events.

The terms that define the community itself can lead to some of the confusion. For a long time, the community was usually referred to as "LGBT," for "lesbian, gay, bisexual, and transgender." At some point, people began to realize that this was too narrow a description and excluded too many people who were obviously part of the community.

Most people then began using "LGBTQ," adding **queer** as an identity. For a lot of people, the Q for "queer" is a catch-all—a way of saying "and everyone else who doesn't fit into the cisgender, heterosexual experience." Asexuality can certainly be considered part of the LGBTQ community when looked at that way.

More Specific Inclusion

Some people have become even more specific, broadening the acronym to LGBTQ+ (where the + indicates "and everyone else") or **LGBTQIA+**, which explicitly includes an "A" for "asexual." Some even longer, more inclusive acronyms are sometimes used (like "LGBTQIA2S+"); from there on, the "A" remains to represent those on the ace spectrum.

Less common but broader acronyms are "SGM" (for "sexual and gender minorities") and "SOGI" (for "sexual orientation and gender identity"). Some people don't want to bother with the acronyms at all and just refer to the entire community as "queer." All of these acronyms implicitly include asexuality.

Many schools now include an LGBTQ group of some sort.

Chapter 3: The Life: Language, Culture, Law, and Community

Finding Community at School

Being aspec can feel a little isolating sometimes, especially for a young person who is figuring it all out while also trying to relate to their peers, but it's possible to find community at school. Many schools now include an LGBTQ group of some sort. Though it may take some explaining to those in the organization, aces certainly fit in any group that works to include and support people who are outside the cisgender, heterosexual experience and the allies of those minority groups.

Sometimes teachers, counselors, and administrators at your school may be well-intentioned but inexperienced in the issues facing ace people. To help them become more educated and more sensitive to the needs of aces, the organization Asexual Outreach has created the Ace Inclusion Guide for High Schools. It gives guidance to the authority figures at schools, as well as to young aces themselves on how to try to make their schools more inclusive. The guide can be found online at https://acesandaros.org/resources/ace-inclusion-guide-for-high-schools.

Representation in Media

Many minority groups have brought awareness to the fact that representation matters. People need to see themselves reflected in the media they consume. Seeing someone who is like oneself depicted in a positive light can be an extremely affirming experience.

As the depiction of other sexual and gender minorities has become more acceptable and common in the dominant culture, asexual representation has lagged behind. In fact, characters who are seen as being less sexual or less sexually successful are often the butt of jokes and just generally not shown positively.

Some of the most prominent asexual characters were never identified explicitly.

Chapter 3: The Life: Language, Culture, Law, and Community

Searching for Aces

Some of the most prominent asexual characters were never identified explicitly as such. For example, Sponge Bob's creators have stated that he was asexual all along, though it's never discussed in the show.

Other examples are characters whom aces have identified as having asexual tendencies that couldn't have been created explicitly with that identity, because they predate the identity. One example of this is Sherlock Holmes. Of course, when Sir Arthur Conan Doyle was writing the Sherlock Holmes mysteries, *asexual* was a word but not an identity. He created a character who didn't seem interested in sex or relationships but never

Some prominent examples of ace's include the character Varys in Game of Thrones.

really had the character discuss that fact, which leaves the door open for modern aces to claim him as one of their own.

More recently, though, works of fiction have begun to make their asexual characters a little clearer. Some prominent examples include the character of Olivia in the Netflix series *Sex Education* and the character Varys in *Game of Thrones.* (Though the latter is a eunuch, he explains that he never had any interest before becoming that way.) One of the most discussed is the character of Todd Chavez in the Netflix series *BoJack Horseman* (see sidebar).

TODD CHAVEZ

Possibly the best representation of asexuality in popular culture up to this point is in a dramedy cartoon that mostly stars animals. In the third season of *BoJack Horseman*, the character of Todd Chavez (voiced by Aaron Paul) comes out to his girlfriend as being asexual.

Later seasons (spoilers ahead) show Todd navigating the world of dating as an asexual. He finds a girlfriend who shares his asexuality, but they break up after they realize that they have nothing else in common. Eventually, Todd finds a girl who shares his asexuality as well as common interests and a similar personality.

Todd Chavez is considered a major step forward in asexual representation in the media. Even though it's a surreal comedy, *BoJack Horseman* tackles some of the important issues that face aces in a way that no show had previously.

Legal Status

Very few laws address asexuality specifically. The only example known to the asexual community is in New York State, which lists asexuals as a protected class. Of course, laws with blanket protections from discrimination because of sexual orientation should cover those on the ace spectrum, but there haven't been any specific cases to test this assumption.

Though social attitudes toward aspecs are still often ignorant and exclusionary, there are no known reports of people being fired or removed from housing because of this sexual orientation, as there have been with other sexual and gender minorities. That doesn't mean it has never happened or that the community should wait until it does happen, though. Asexual advocates are already working to make sure that asexuals are explicitly included in legally protected groups.

TEXT-DEPENDENT QUESTIONS

1. Describe the ace flag and what it represents.
2. What is AVEN? What role does it fill in the asexual community?
3. What does a black ring on the right middle finger represent?

RESEARCH PROJECTS

1. After watching the video The Rise of Asexual Representation (https://www.youtube.com/watch?v=FV7C4xos5pY), describe two depictions of asexuality in media and how accurately or inaccurately they present asexuality the community.
2. Find as many terms as you can that define the broader sexual minority community (e.g., LGBTQ, queer). There are more than those discussed here! Which do you think represents the community best? Why?

Asexuality was once treated as a disorder or dysfunction.

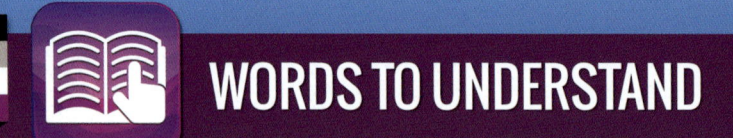

WORDS TO UNDERSTAND

Disorder: A condition that disrupts normal function and causes emotional distress.

Hormones: Molecules produced in glands in order to control another part of the body.

Hypoactive sexual desire disorder (HSDD): A condition that asexuals have mistakenly been diagnosed with, in which sex drive is suppressed due to circumstances outside of sexual orientation.

CHAPTER 4

TAKING CARE OF YOURSELF: HEALTH AND MEDICINE

Over the decades, many theories have arisen that try to explain away asexuality as something that's wrong with a person instead of something that is an innate, natural part of who they are. Asexuality was treated as a **disorder** or dysfunction, whether biological or psychological.

The thought of the psychological establishment was that either there was something in a person's body that wasn't working right or that some trauma or abuse had turned them off from having a "normal" sex drive. The more people understand about asexuality, the less sense these theories make.

Asexual Bodies and Minds Are Normal

Research on asexuality is still in its early years, but the work that has been done seems to disprove the theory that there is something biologically wrong with asexual people.

A 2011 study conducted by Lori Brotto and Morag Yule demonstrated that asexual and allosexual women's bodies respond similarly to sexual stimuli. *Biologically*, then, asexuals

Biologically, *asexuals seem to be the same as allosexuals.*

seem to be the same as allosexuals. The difference is the feeling of sexual attraction. That's an important part of why asexuality is a sexual orientation and not a sexual dysfunction.

Similarly, though no extensive research has been done on the subject, there's no reason to think that aces have a higher-than-normal rate of trauma—sexual or otherwise. As that has been a topic of conversation on discussion boards, many members of the ace community have shared that they have nothing in their lives that would explain their asexuality from a psychological angle.

HSDD is an umbrella term for anything that can decrease a person's sex drive.

HSDD Causes Distress; Asexuality Does Not

There is a condition called **hypoactive sexual desire disorder (HSDD)**, which some people have tried to associate with asexuality. HSDD is an umbrella term for anything that can decrease a person's sex drive. It can be a result of a hormone imbalance, a reaction to a medication, a side effect of depression and anxiety, or the result of a wide range of other factors. Some have used the existence of this disorder as evidence that asexuality is caused by something specific that is wrong with them, instead of just their sexual orientation.

The biggest reason that asexuality cannot be considered a disorder, though, is that aces don't feel a loss by not feeling sexual attraction. In order for something to be considered a disorder, it has to cause emotional distress.

If a person loses their sex drive at some point and is very upset about that fact, that would likely be considered HSDD. If a person has never felt the type of sexual attraction that allosexuals do and is generally content with that fact, that is asexuality.

Although asexuality has been misdiagnosed as HSDD many times, HSDD is also a real thing. If you think that a physical or emotional issue may be impairing your sex drive, and you would like to do something about it, it might be a good idea to seek the advice of a doctor.

Hormones

Since a hormone imbalance is one of the factors that can lead to HSDD, many doctors and psychologists through the years have assumed that asexuality is caused by a hormone imbalance.

What is a **hormone**? The broadest definition is that a hormone is a molecule that is produced in a gland and then transported through the body to control another part. For

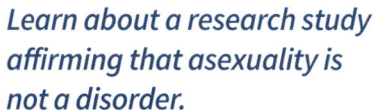

Learn about a research study affirming that asexuality is not a disorder.

example, the pituitary gland produces hormones that move throughout your body to control metabolism, reproduction, and much more.

A lot of sexual behavior is governed by hormones. For men, testosterone is the most important hormone for sexual motivation, and low testosterone is often found in allosexual men who have experienced a drop in sex drive.

For women, estrogen, progesterone, and, to a lesser degree, testosterone are the most important reproductive hormones. High estrogen levels can increase sexual interest, while high progesterone levels have the opposite effect. The role of testosterone in sexual interest in women is less understood.

Chapter 4: Taking Care of Yourself: Health and Medicine   65

Estrogen

Estrone (E1)
$C_{18}H_{22}O_2$

Estradiol (E2)
$C_{18}H_{24}O_2$

Estriol (E3)
$C_{18}H_{24}O_3$

Estetrol (E4)

No scientific research has yet been conducted on the hormone levels of asexuals.

Hormones and Asexuality

No scientific research has yet been conducted on the hormone levels of asexuals. But many aces have received hormone-level tests from their doctors on their own and shared the results on the AVEN forum. Some of those who have shared their results have found that their hormone levels vary from the average, but many have been told by their doctors that theirs are within what would be considered normal.

It's worth noting that a portion of any group is going to receive results that aren't typical. If the proportion of those people is higher in the asexual community, it is something that needs to be studied. It does seem clear, though, that there is not a direct correlation between hormone levels and asexuality, since so many have found that their levels are normal.

Asexuality and Mental Health

Aces, like other sexual and gender minorities, still face a lot of stigmatizing from society at large. Allosexuals often just don't understand an asexual perspective, and often people aren't particularly interested in trying to understand something unfamiliar to them. This attitude can lead to aces feeling excluded from many social situations.

This feeling of rejection can have a very negative effect on a person's mental health. That fact has been documented countless times among other LGBTQ people. The available research on asexuals specifically indicates that they, too, experience the negative mental effects of rejection by the larger society.

As a result, aces are reported to have higher-than-average rates of depression and anxiety. If you find yourself feeling anxious or depressed, that is a normal response to the issues that face aspecs and other gender and sexual minorities. There are many others who feel the same way or have at some point felt the same way. That is why having a sense of community can be helpful (see chapter 3).

Other resources that might help are counseling or talking to a friend or authority figure. For one resource specifically for LGBTQ youth, check out the sidebar on the Trevor Project.

The Trevor Project has been helping young LGBTQ people since 1998.

THE TREVOR PROJECT

The Trevor Project has been helping young people within the LGBTQ community since 1998. The organization provides counseling services 24/7 over the phone and through text, email, and instant messaging on its website. It also runs a social media forum for people to interact with each other.

The Trevor Project specifically lists those on the asexual spectrum as one of the communities that it serves. If you feel that you need emotional support, especially if you find yourself thinking about self-harm or suicide, go to thetrevorproject.org to find help, or contact the organization in one of these ways:

- By phone: Trevor Lifeline: 866-488-7386
- By texting "START" to 678678 for TrevorText
- Through chat by visiting TrevorChat.org
- On the social media platform at TrevorSpace.org

Substance Abuse

No research has been done yet on drug and alcohol use among the ace community, but the depression and anxiety that are caused by stigma and lack of understanding are common risk factors for addiction and substance abuse. The LGBTQ community as a whole struggles with this issue as a result. It's something to be aware of and cautious about as you come to understand yourself more and begin to form your community. If you find yourself struggling with addiction or drug or alcohol abuse, get help from friends, family, counselors, or resources like the Trevor Project.

No research has been done yet on drug and alcohol use among the ace community.

Two important issues are sexually transmitted infections as well as pregnancy.

Sexual Health

It may seem strange to include a section on sexual health in a book about asexuality, but just because someone is asexual, that does not mean that they are a lifelong virgin. Many aces choose to have sex at some point in their lives, whether for a partner, the sake of curiosity, or any number of other reasons.

It's important to remember that a person's risk to their sexual health is based upon their behavior, not their identity. Sometimes, if a person has a particular identity, that is what they have in mind when they hear about sexual health. A person may be told something about risk factors and think, "Well that doesn't apply to me." Then later, when the situation arises, they may be unprepared to protect themselves.

Two important issues are STIs (sexually transmitted infections) as well as pregnancy. The identity of a person with a womb may lead them to believe that they don't need to ever worry about becoming pregnant, but when experimentation happens, unplanned pregnancies can result.

Make sure that you know your risks based upon your behavior. It's also always helpful to be aware of sexual health issues in general. Don't take for granted what information applies to you and what doesn't.

TEXT-DEPENDENT QUESTIONS

1. How does a person's asexuality affect their sexual risk?
2. Describe HSDD. Why have people confused it with asexuality?
3. What is the difference between HSDD and asexuality?

RESEARCH PROJECTS

1. Learn more about hormones. How do they affect a person's sex drive? How do they affect a person's emotions and state of mind?
2. Very little research has been done on the health and psychology of asexuals, compared to those of other sexual orientations and groups of people. What types of research do you think would be most helpful? What would be a good way to conduct that research?

Coming out has become shorthand for telling people about your sexual orientation.

WORDS TO UNDERSTAND

Coming out: An expression that refers to the process of telling others an aspect of our identity that they didn't know previously, usually in regard to sexual orientation or gender identity.

Disclosure: Making information known that was not previously known.

Frame of reference: A perspective on an issue, drawing from past experience with it.

CHAPTER 5

COMING OUT: A PERSONAL DECISION

Cairo Kennedy, who runs *The Demisexual: A Demisexual Lifestyle Blog* (thedemisexual.com), describes the way her outlook on life has changed since embracing her identity:

> I have the confidence to own my demisexuality.
> I've learned that I don't have to be in a relationship to be a complete and valuable person.
> Since embracing the label, I've learnt how to say no and become comfortable enforcing my boundaries without worrying about the consequences. I've figured out how to say that I want to get to know someone better before the relationship takes a physical turn.
> Being demisexual has taught me I'm not broken, and it's completely valid for me to not only enforce my boundaries but to insist that people respect them, even if they don't understand.

What It Means to Come Out

Coming out has become shorthand for telling the people around you about your sexual orientation or gender identity. It's short for "coming out of the closet," which is something that began in the LGBTQ community to use the image of someone coming out of hiding.

Coming out is a personal process that happens differently for each person. You can decide what coming out looks like for you. You're not obligated to tell anyone, but you may choose to do so to help friends, family, and the people you interact with to understand you a little better.

Coming Out to Yourself

The first part of the coming-out process is coming to terms with your sexuality in your own mind. Sometimes that can be the

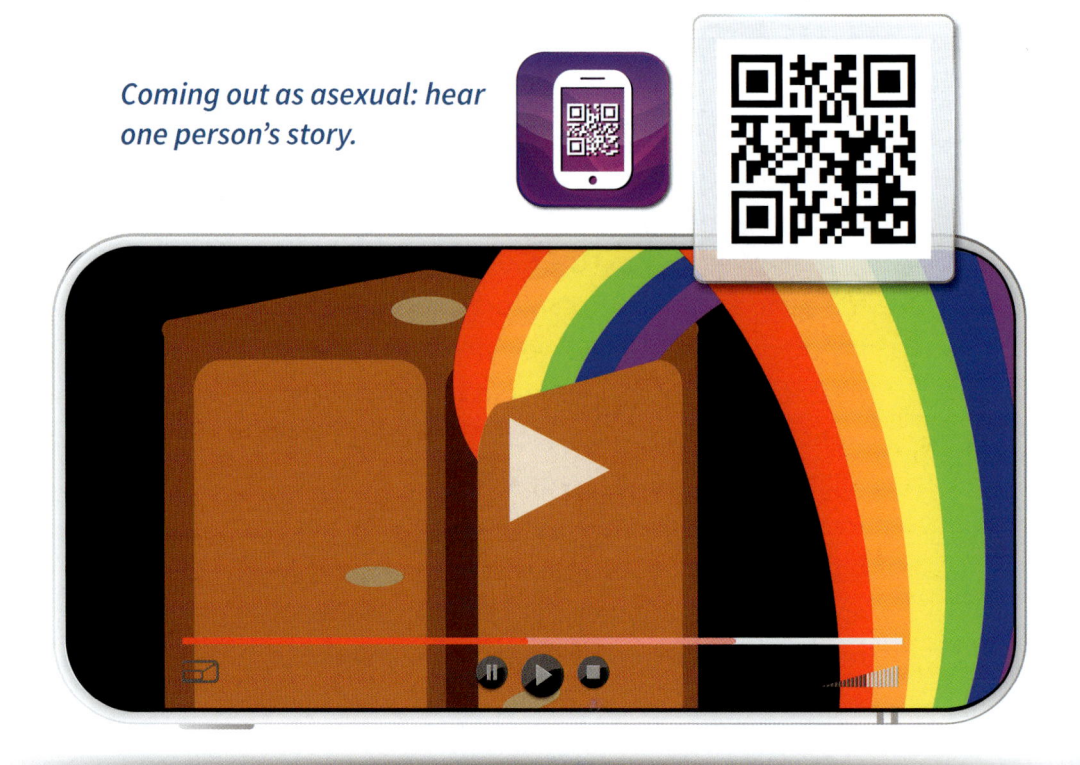

Coming out as asexual: hear one person's story.

hardest part. It takes emotional work and self-awareness for a person to figure out who they are and what is best for them. It can be scary to realize that your sexuality is different from that of others, but it's an important and rewarding step.

Sometimes this is also the longest part of the process. It's not a race, and it's not something that you have to complete by a deadline. It's often something that takes time. Some people seem to know exactly who they are right away. Most people have to really work on it.

Coming Out to the Aspec Community

Many people begin exploring the ace community online even before coming out to themselves. They just realize that there's something different about them but can't really put their finger on what that difference is. Reading about the experiences of others sometimes helps people put words to what they are feeling.

As mentioned previously, the AVEN forum boards have helped many people explore their sexual and romantic orientations. Some find that they relate to the experience of asexuals, gray-asexuals, demisexuals, or one of the other identities that people have described there. They may discover that none of those potential labels really fits them.

If a person does find that they relate to one of the labels, often the first people they come out to are those in the forum. That can be good practice for the potentially difficult conversations to come later. It's a way to share something about yourself to a welcoming and sympathetic audience.

Coming Out to Friends and Family

For many, **disclosure** to their friends and family is the scariest part of the process. Those closest to us are often those who have the strongest opinions about our lives. While there's no need to assume the worst about how people will react, it's good to be

Many people begin exploring the ace community online.

prepared for what you will do if the response isn't as positive as you would like. For some ideas on how to handle a wide range of different coming-out scenarios, check out the Trevor Project's *Coming Out Handbook* mentioned in the sidebar.

There's no "best" way to come out that fits everyone, including the order of people to talk to. Maybe you'll want to come out to your friends first, because you think they'll be the most supportive. Maybe you'll want to come out to your family first, because you're closest to them. Maybe for you, it's best to start with a trusted authority figure who can help you through the process.

Most people don't have a frame of reference regarding asexuality.

The Special Challenge of Coming Out As Ace

Those on the asexual spectrum have a special hurdle to leap: people's ignorance of what asexuality is. When someone comes out as gay, lesbian, or bisexual, people know what that means. They have some frame of reference to understand what that person is telling them.

Most people don't have a **frame of reference** regarding asexuality. Some may not be familiar with the word at all. Some may have misconceptions about what it means. Some may even believe that asexuality doesn't exist, which can be especially frustrating. You've worked up the courage to share part of yourself with someone, but then that person thinks that you're making it up.

In this situation, patience may be needed, along with a certain amount of explanation. It's not your job to educate everyone around you, but you may find it beneficial to take the time to explain it to those you care about most. If you don't feel equipped to do so, AVEN has a very useful resource to which you can point people that may help them understand, an FAQ specifically for friends and family (see sidebar).

Discussing Your Romantic Orientation

It's up to you if you want to discuss your romantic orientation when you tell people about your sexual orientation. You don't have to if you don't want to, but be prepared for questions. Often, one of the first questions when an ace comes out is, "Does this mean you're going to be single forever?" or some variation on that.

It's wise to have a response to that question prepared for when it comes up, whether or not that means fully explaining the spectrum of romantic orientation. It's also perfectly valid to

SOME RESOURCES FOR COMING OUT

The Trevor Project has created a great resource for helping people think through the entire process of coming out: *The Coming Out Handbook*. You can find it at https://www.thetrevorproject.org/resources/guide/the-coming-out-handbook/ or by going to thetrevorproject.org and clicking on "Resources."

AVEN has created a special FAQ for friends and family of people who have come out as ace. You may find it useful in dispelling some of the myths and misconceptions about asexuality. You can find it at https://www.asexuality.org/?q=family.html or by going to asexuality.org and clicking on "About Asexuality" and then on "Friends/Family FAQ."

tell people that you don't know the answer to that question yet. Sometimes "I'm figuring things out" is a hard answer for people to accept, but if that is the honest answer, they'll need to learn to accept it.

Coming Out to a Potential Partner

Another special challenge for aspecs is having the conversation about asexuality with a potential partner. As discussed, not all asexuals are aromantic. Many hope to have a relationship at some point. Gray-asexuals and demisexuals may just need to have a certain set of circumstances met in a relationship for sexual attraction to come. That means having to let someone know, preferably up front, what they can expect from dating you or having a relationship with you, and it can make for some awkward

Many asexuals hope to have a relationship at some point.

first dates if the information hasn't been shared before. Some aspecs prefer to get it out of the way in the initial interaction when the first-date plans are made, before the date even starts.

Many on the ace spectrum, particularly demisexuals, would prefer to have some degree of relationship with the potential partner before the first date even comes. In those cases, presumably the person will know them well enough to already know about their asexuality. Even when that is the case, though, having a clear and honest conversation is still a good idea.

At some point in their dating lives (should they choose to have one), most aspecs will have an experience in which their date knows that they are asexual, promises that they're okay

For aces, there are some advantages to finding dates through apps.

Chapter 5: Coming Out: A Personal Decision

with it, and then later is surprised that sexual contact doesn't happen when they want it to. Other times, people think that they're going to "fix" an asexual with what they consider to be their irresistibility. These aren't things that should discourage you from dating if you want to, they're just things to be aware of as you enter the dating world.

The Advantages and Disadvantages of Modern Dating

Many on the ace spectrum prefer to date someone they have established a relationship with before the romantic part begins, but that isn't always possible. Many dating apps and websites have sprung up to fill that hole. The drawbacks of these apps are well known. A certain amount of anonymity can make people think they can act in ways they never would in public. They can make it even easier for people to misrepresent themselves.

For aces, there are some advantages to finding dates through apps (once they're old enough to use them). Some apps, like Tinder, have a pretty comprehensive list of sexual orientations and gender identities to choose from as part of a profile. Even those that don't have that feature will allow you to include that information in the text of your profile. The reason that is an advantage is that it allows you to communicate what to expect from dating you before first contact even occurs. There's no excuse for being surprised by a person's asexuality when it was front and center on their profile. It can also help aces find other aces in their local area in a way that isn't always possible through global messaging boards.

Choosing Not to Come Out

You are not obligated to share anything personal with anyone if you don't want to. Unfortunately, coming out as something that

Some aces are perfectly happy without the complications of sex and relationships.

isn't cisgender and heterosexual isn't safe for some. Some aces, particularly acearos, just don't feel the need to tell the people around them about their sexual orientation. They're perfectly happy just going through life without the complications of sex and relationships while also avoiding the complications of having conversations about it.

    At the end of the day, your decision of whether or not to come out and (if you decide to) how to do so is entirely up to you. The chances are good that after some careful thought and consideration, you'll know what's best to do in your situation.

On the Other Side

Coming to terms with sexual orientation, romantic orientation, gender identity, and all of the other parts that make someone who they are is a great challenge for us all. Although you will always be learning more about yourself, there can be a point where you'll feel like you're on the right track. Pain and confusion can give way to comfort in your own skin.

"It was hard to come to terms with being asexual," college student Charlie King told GLAAD. "I felt broken and like no one would want to be with me. For a long time, I thought there was something medically wrong with me. I have grown from what I initially felt when I realized my sexuality and now think that it's great that I can connect with my partner on different levels that don't involve sex. While it can still be a challenge to meet people who are also asexual, I know that I will find the right person and have a great community around me."

TEXT-DEPENDENT QUESTIONS

1. What does it mean to "come out"?
2. What are the special challenges of coming out as someone on the asexual spectrum?
3. How can online and app-based dating work in aces' favor?

RESEARCH PROJECT

Find three ace coming-out stories online—written or video. What similarities are there among their stories? How did their experiences vary?

SERIES GLOSSARY OF KEY TERMS

Acearo: A person who identifies as both asexual ("ace") and aromantic ("aro").
Aesthetic attraction: A nonsexual appreciation of a person's appearance.
Agender: Referring to a person who does not identify themselves as having a particular gender.
Allosexual: Someone who feels sexual attraction to other people.
Ally: A person who is not a member of a marginalized group but who gives support to that group.
Aromantic: Referring to a sexual orientation in which a person is not interested in forming a romantic relationship.
Asexual: Referring to a sexual orientation in which a person is not sexually attracted to anyone.
Aspec: A way to refer to the asexual spectrum and those on it.
Assigned female at birth (AFAB): Born with genitals visually consistent with female physiology.
Assigned male at birth (AMAB): Born with genitals visually consistent with male physiology.
AVEN: Asexuality Visibility and Education Network.
Binder: A special garment that transmasculine individuals wear in order to compress their chest and achieve a more masculine profile.
Biphobia: Fear of bisexuality or people who identify as bisexual.
Bodily autonomy: A person's right to make the decisions about their own body.
Bottom surgery: An umbrella term that refers to several different lower surgeries designed to align an AFAB individual's body with their gender identity. These procedures include hysterectomy, oophorectomy, metoidioplasty, and phalloplasty.
Butch: A gender presentation that could be considered masculine.
Chondrolaryngoplasty: A surgical procedure that reduces the size and visibility of the thyroid cartilage, also known as the *Adam's apple*.
Chosen family: A system of close bonds, via friendship or romantic relationship, from which a person constructs a nonbiological "family" unit.
Chromosomes: The structures containing genes in cells; intersex traits are usually found on the X or Y chromosome.
Cisgender: Referring to a person who feels generally comfortable in, and identifies as, the gender they were assigned at birth.
Cisnormative: Referring to the assumption that cisgender as a category is normal and central, and that any experience that differs from it is abnormal.
Clitorectomy: The surgical removal of a clitoris.
Coming out: A common shorthand for "coming out of the closet," the process by which an individual reveals their gender identity or sexual orientation to others.
Consensual: Agreed to and mutually understood between or among both or all involved members or parties.

Conversion therapy: Any attempt to alter a person's sexual orientation, gender identity, or gender expression. This practice is banned in many countries and states.

Deadname: A transgender person's birth name. While not everyone refers to their birth name in this way, the term *deadname* represents the complex feelings that many transgender people have about their birth names. When used as a verb, *deadnaming* refers to the practice of using a trans person's birth name after they have changed it.

Demisexual: Referring to a sexual orientation in which a person is only sexually attracted to someone after forming a deep emotional bond.

Enby: A nickname for "nonbinary" that comes from its abbreviation (NB).

Estrogen: A hormone that promotes and maintains biologically female characteristics.

Feminine-of-center: The experience of feeling closer to a traditionally feminine gender experience on the spectrum of gendered experiences and behaviors.

Femme: A gender presentation that could be considered feminine.

Foreplay: Acts that occur before advanced sexual behavior occurs, such as flirting, massaging, kissing, or cuddling.

Gatekeeping: The practice of creating barriers to the access of gender-affirming care. Examples include requiring that patients get a recommendation from a therapist in order to receive hormones or surgeries, delaying care or referral to other providers without sufficient medical justification, or requiring that patients have a binary gender identity or presentation in order to receive gender-affirming treatment.

Gender affirmation surgery: Procedures that assist in a person's medical transition to their correct gender identity.

Gender-affirming: A health care principle that treats a person holistically, recognizing the impact that their gender identity or sexual experience may have on the treatment they receive. This is widely recognized as best medical practice.

Gender binary: The concept of gender having only two options: female and male.

Gender dysphoria: The discomfort a person feels as a result of gender incongruence. This may take the form of social dysphoria, body dysphoria, or both. *See also* **gender incongruence**.

Gender essentialism: The idea that a person's gender is determined by their biology rather than a matter of personal and social identity.

Gender euphoria: The positive feelings a person experiences because of being seen or treated in accordance with their gender identity.

Gender expansive: An umbrella term for anyone whose gender does not match the gender they were assigned at birth, whether that is the opposite gender or somewhere in the middle.

Gender expression: The way a person presents gender outwardly, through behavior, clothing, voice, or other characteristics.

Gender identity: A person's internal sense of their gender.

Gender incongruence: The mismatch a person perceives between their assigned sex at birth and their gender identity. *See also* **gender dysphoria**.

Gender nonconforming: Referring to someone who doesn't live by traditional gender rules; can also be used as a synonym for *gender expansive*.

SERIES GLOSSARY OF KEY TERMS

Genderfluid: When a person's gender identity moves freely across the gender spectrum.

Genderqueer: A person who rejects the binary male-female categories of gender; they may identify as some combination of female and male, or no gender at all.

Gray-asexual: Referring to a sexual orientation in which a person feels a very limited sexual attraction, often only within very specific circumstances.

Heterocentrism: An assumption (often unconscious) that everyone is heterosexual, and the attitudes and social structures that result in that assumption.

Heterosexual: Attracted exclusively to people of the opposite gender. From the Greek *heteros*, which means "the other of two things."

Homosexual: Attracted exclusively to people of the same gender. From the Greek *homos*, which means "same."

Hormone replacement therapy (HRT): Also called *gender-affirming hormone therapy* (GAHT), HRT is a therapeutic medical process where hormones are administered to alter a person's appearance to bring it closer to their gender identity.

Identity invalidation: Refusing to see an individual's sexuality as valid.

Informed consent: An affirmative, patient-led approach to transgender care in which adults and legally emancipated minors are educated on the benefits, limitations, and risks of gender-affirming treatments and are allowed to make an informed decision about whether to pursue them without the need for the recommendation of a mental health provider.

Intersex: Any of around 30 physical differences that make a person biologically outside of what is generally considered "typical" of a female or male body.

LGBTQIA+: A more inclusive acronym that includes gay, lesbian, bisexual, transgender, queer, intersex, asexual, and all other sex or gender identities.

Masc: A gender presentation that could be considered masculine.

Masculine-of-center: The experience of feeling closer to a traditionally masculine gender experience on the spectrum of gendered experiences and behaviors.

Misgender (verb): When someone intentionally or unintentionally refers to a trans person in a way that does not align with their gender identity. This can happen through the use of incorrect pronouns, gendered honorifics like *Miss* or *Ms.*, or inappropriately gendered terminology such as *waitress* or *actress*.

Non-traditional family: Any family dynamic that does not fit the traditional model of one man and one woman who are married to each other and raising kids together.

Nonbinary: An umbrella term for gender identities that are neither male nor female—identities that are outside the gender binary.

Nonconsensual: Referring to something that has not been agreed to by everyone involved.

Outing: Exposing someone's LGBTQIA+ identity without their permission.

Packer: A prosthetic device that transmasculine individuals wear to create the appearance of a natural bulge in their pants.

Pansexual: Referring to a person who can be attracted to a person of any gender, or a person for whom gender is not an important factor in their attraction to a person.

Asexual

Passing privilege: The relative social ease that comes from a transgender person's ability to be read as cisgender.
Perceived gender: The gender that a person is assumed to have, based on external characteristics and behaviors.
Queer: Sometimes used as a general term for all sexual and gender minorities.
Romantic attraction: Attraction that makes people desire a romantic connection with someone else.
Sexual attraction: Attraction that makes someone desire sexual contact with, or show sexual interest in, another person.
Sexual orientation: An identity (independent of gender identity) that expresses whom someone is sexually attracted to.
Sexually transmitted infection (STI): Viruses and bacteria that can be passed from person to person during intimate contact.
Social transition: The process by which a trans or gender-diverse person adopts the name, pronouns, and presentation that suit their gender identity.
Stealth (adjective): A slang term that refers to an individual who has chosen not to disclose that they are transgender.
STP: A "stand-to-pee" device that resembles a penis that transmasculine people use to pee standing up.
Straight privilege: Unconscious, taken-for-granted benefits afforded to straight people in a heterosexist society due to their sexual orientation.
Testosterone: A hormone that affects sex characteristics and reproduction.
Threesome: A relationship that involves three people; the three-person equivalent of a two-person couple.
Title IX: A federal law that prohibits discrimination on the basis of sex in any educational programs or activities, expanded recently to include discrimination on the basis of sexual orientation or gender identity.
To pass (or be read) as a gender: To be seen as the gender a person identifies as, typically by people who are not aware that they are transgender.
Top surgery: A surgical procedure involving the removal of the breasts, the purpose of which is to align an AFAB individual's body with their gender identity.
Transfeminine: An identity denoting when a person's gender identity or expression skews partially or fully feminine and differs from their assigned sex at birth.
Transgender: Someone who identifies with the opposite end of the gender binary than the one they were assigned at birth; can also be used as a synonym for *gender expansive*.
Transmasculine: Referring to a person assigned female at birth (AFAB) who identifies with masculinity.
Transmisogyny: The intersection of transphobia and misogyny, a form of misogyny specifically directed at trans women and transfeminine people.
Transphobia: The stigma and discrimination that transgender people face for being transgender or for deviating from gender norms.
Vaginoplasty: The surgical construction or reforming of a vagina.

FURTHER READING & INTERNET RESOURCES

BOOKS

Bogaert, Anthony, F. *Understanding Asexuality.* Washington, D.C.: Rowman & Littlefield, 2015.
Although an influential book, and one of the first academic books published about asexuality, it is somewhat controversial within the ace community. Some feel that it speaks to their experience; others feel that it's too much of an outsider's perspective.

Burgess, Rebecca. *How to Be Ace: A Memoir of Growing Up Asexual.* London: Jessica Kingsley, 2020.
A graphic novel memoir about the author and artist coming of age while discovering their asexual identity.

Chen, Angela. *Ace: What Asexuality Reveals about Desire, Society, and the Meaning of Sex.* Boston: Beacon Press, 2020.
The title makes it seem somewhat emotionally detached, but it includes some very personal stories from the author as well as a diverse group of other aces, including "disabled aces, aces of color, gender-nonconforming aces, and aces who both do and don't want romantic relationships."

Decker, Julie Sondra. *The Invisible Orientation: An Introduction to Asexuality.* New York: Skyhorse, 2015.
Written by an acearo woman, this book provides an overview of the asexual experience and community. Comprehensive and well-researched, without being too academic in tone.

Hopkinson, Elizabeth, and Anna Hopkinson. *Asexual Fairy Tales.* Bristol, UK: SilverWood Books, 2019.
A collection of classic stories and mythological tales that include asexual characters and asexual themes. Not all fairy tales involve a princess waiting for her prince.

WEBSITES

Aces & Aros (www.acesandaros.org)
Part of Asexual Outreach, Aces & Aros provides information about local events. It is also the site that hosts the Ace Inclusion Guide for High Schools.

Asexual Outreach (www.asexualoutreach.org)
Asexual Outreach is an advocacy and community organization that works for the ace and aro community. This group is responsible for organizing Ace Week. Information about Ace Week events can be found on its website.

AVEN: Asexual Visibility and Education Network (www.asexuality.org)
The official site of AVEN, this is every ace's first stop on the Internet. It provides a wealth of informational resources and the most active asexual forum online.

Demisexual Lifestyle Blog (www.thedemisexual.com)
A well-known lifestyle blog written by Cairo Kennedy, the *Demisexual Lifestyle Blog* includes blog posts about life as a demisexual, as well as dating, relationships, and more.

LGBTQ Task Force (www.thetaskforce.org)
The National LGBTQ Task Force is an advocacy group that works for the rights of all queer people. Here you can stay informed on what's happening right now in the fight for LGBTQIA rights.

Sounds Fake But Okay (www.soundsfakepod.com)
The official website of the podcast *Sounds Fake But Okay*. You can listen to episodes of the podcast and find some ace and aro swag, as well as a wide variety of resources for accessing the aspec community.

The Trevor Project (www.thetrevorproject.org)
The Trevor Project has many resources for LGBTQ youth of all types, with explicit inclusion of those on the asexual spectrum, including *The Coming Out Handbook*. It offers free counseling services via phone, text, and chat.

INDEX

abstinence, 22–23
Ace (Chen), 92
acearo, 28, 39
Ace Inclusion Guide for High Schools, 54
aces, 16. *See also* asexual
Aces & Aros, 93
Ace Week, 50–51
addiction, 69–70
aesthetic attraction, 28, 32–33
agender identity, 40
alcohol, 69–70
allosexual, 28, 61–63
allosexuals, 61–63
anxiety, 67–68
aromantic, 12, 21
arousal, 33–34
asexual
    attitude toward sex, 23–26
    combining identities, 38–39
    coming out as, 80–81
    concepts surrounding, 16–17, 22–23
    crushes, 32–33
    discussion, 12–16
    gray-asexual orientation, 34, 36
    hormones and, 60, 64–67
    LGBTQ community and, 52–54
    relationships, 19–21
    representation in media, 54–57
    self-identification, 30–32, 40
    signs and symbols, 47–51
    special events, 50–51
Asexual Fairy Tales (Hopkinson & Hopkinson), 92
Asexuality Archive, 49
Asexuality Awareness Week, 51
Asexual Outreach, 93
Asexual Visibility and Education Network (AVEN)
    coming out resources, 77, 80–81, 93
    community, 44–51, 53
    terminology originating with, 39, 47
aspec, 28. *See also* asexual

baby boomers, 9
Benoit, Yasmin, 13
bisexual, 44
bisexual orientation, 13, 16, 21
Bogaert, Anthony, F., 92
BoJack Horseman, 57
Brotto, Lori, 61
Burgess, Rebecca, 92

celibacy, 22–23
Chavez, Todd (character), 57
Chen, Angela, 92
chromosomes, 7
combining identities, 38–41
coming out
    to aspec community, 77–78
    dating and, 81–84

    decision on, 84–86
    discussion, 74–76
    to friends and family, 77–79
    to oneself first, 76–77
    to potential partner, 81–84
    resources, 79–81
    special challenges for aces, 80
Coming Out Handbook, 79, 93
community
    discussion, 44–49
    mental health and, 67–68
Costello, Sarah, 48
crushes, 32–33

dating, 81–84
Decker, Julie Sondra, 92
demisexual
    determining if one is, 36–37
    discussion, 12, 18–19, 26, 38
    origin of term, 39, 47
Demisexual Lifestyle Blog, 75, 93
depression, 67–68
disclosure, 74, 77–78
disorders, 60–61, 63–64
Doyle, Arthur Conan, 56
drugs, 69–70

estrogen, 65–66
events, 50–51

fantasies, 34–35
flag, 49–50, 53
frame of reference, 74, 79–80

Game of Thrones, 56–57
gay, 44
gender identity, 6–11, 40–41
genderqueer identity, 40
Generation Z, 9
GLAAD, 45, 86
gray-asexual
    attitude toward sex, 23–26
    determining if one is, 34, 36
    discussion, 12, 17, 26
    origin of term, 47
    physical relationships, 23
    sexual contact, 23

health
    discussion, 60–61
    hormones, 60, 64–67
    HSDD, 60–61, 63–64
    mental, 67–68
    sexual, 71–72
    STIs, 71–72
    substance abuse, 69–70
heterosexual orientation, 13, 16, 21
Holmes, Sherlock (character), 56–57

homosexual orientation, 13, 16, 21
Hopkinson, Anna, 92
Hopkinson, Elizabeth, 92
hormones, 60, 64–67
How to Be Ace (Burgess), 92
hypoactive sexual desire disorder (HSDD), 60–61, 63–64

International Asexuality Day, 50–51
Invisible Orientation, The (Decker), 92

Jay, David, 45–46

Kaszyca, Kayla, 48
Kennedy, Cairo, 75
King, Charlie, 86

labels, 29–30
language, 44–45
law, 44–45, 58
lesbian, 44
LGBTQ, 44, 49, 52–53, 68–69, 81
LGBTQIA, 9
LGBTQIA+, 44, 52
LGBTQ Task Force, 93
libido, 28, 61–67

marriage, 10–11, 20, 50
masturbation, 33–34
media representations, 54–57
medicine, 60–61
mental health, 67–68

neuroscience, 7
New York, 58

Orr, Addie, 45

pansexual, 15, 21
patience, 29–30, 42
Paul, Aaron, 57
physical relationships, 23. *See also* sexual contact
polyamorous relationships, 8, 11
potential partner, 81–84
pregnancy, 71–72
Pride events, 52
progesterone, 65–66

QR Video
    asexual activist on sexual attraction myths, 51
    asexuality research, 65
    asexual persons explain meaning of term, 32
    coming out story, 76
    David Jay on asexuality, 16
    demisexual persons on meaning of term, 38

queer, 44, 52
queerplatonic, 28, 37

rainbow flag, 49, 53
relationships. *See also* sexual contact
    asexuality and, 19–21
    changing ideas on, 10–11
    physical, 23
    polyamorous, 8, 11
research projects, 27, 43, 59, 73
resources, 68–69, 77, 79–81, 93
right to marry laws, 10–11
ring, 50
Roddenberry, Gene, 6
romantic orientation, 21, 80–81

Savin-Williams, Ritch, 34
school community, 53–54, 93
self-identification
    coming out to oneself, 76–77
    discussion, 9, 28–29
    patience during process of, 29–30, 42
sex-averse attitude, 23–26
sex drive, 61–67
Sex Education, 57
sex-favorable attitude, 23–26
sex-indifferent attitude, 23–26
sex-repulsed attitude, 23–26
sexual and gender minorities (SGM), 52
sexual attraction, 6–11, 51
sexual contact, 23–26, 36–37
sexual health, 71–72
sexually transmitted infections (STIs), 71–72
sexual orientation, 12–15, 40–41. *See also specific orientations*
sexual orientation and gender identity (SOGI), 52
SGM (sexual and gender minorities), 52
signs, 47–51
Sounds Fake But Okay podcast, 48, 93
special events, 50–51
Sponge Bob (character), 55–56
STIs (sexually transmitted infections), 71–72
substance abuse, 69–70
Supreme Court, 10–11
symbols, 47–51

testosterone, 65–66
transgender, 44
Trevor Project, 68–69, 79, 81, 93

Understanding Asexuality (Bogaert), 92

Varys (character), 56–57

Yule, Morag, 61

Index 95

AUTHOR'S BIOGRAPHY

Jeremy Quist is an author, academic, and California native. He conducted academic research on LGBTQ identity and community in Eastern Europe while earning an MS in international development. Jeremy has continued to write about the LGBTQ community since then, including three volumes of Mason Crest's LGBTQ Life series. He has lived throughout the western United States.

CREDITS

COVER

mimagephotography/Shutterstock

INTERIOR

7, Geartooth Productions/Shutterstock; 8, Sangiao Photography/Shutterstock; 10, DisobeyArt/Shutterstock; 12, Viktor Lom/Shutterstock; 14, StasyKID/Shutterstock; 16, Vasara/Shutterstock; 18, NDAB Creativity/Shutterstock; 20, Nadav Garb/Shutterstock; 22, fizkes/Shutterstock; 24,4 PM production/Shutterstock; 25, Lucky Business/Shutterstock; 28, Jan H Anderson/Shutterstock; 31, solominviktor/Shutterstock; 32, artfury/Shutterstock; 33, Thomas Adnre Fure/Shutterstock; 35, DIMITRII SIMAKOV/Shutterstock; 37, Cat Act Art/Shutterstock; 38, droid photo/Shutterstock; 41, Alberto Menendez Cervero/Shutterstock; 44, shiftdrive/Shutterstock; 46, Rawpixel.com/Shutterstock; 48, Stock-Asso/Shutterstock; 49, Maxim Studio/Shutterstock; 51, enterlinedesign/Shutterstock; 53, Menno van der Haven/Shutterstock; 55, lev radin/Shutterstock; 56, New Vision/Shutterstock; 60, Semachkovsky/Shutterstock; 62, Anna_An/Shutterstock; 63, Sklo Studio/Shutterstock; 65, Margarita Young/Shutterstock; 66, Ekaterina Minaeva/Shutterstock; 68, Lee Snider Photo Images/Shutterstock; 70, monticello/Shutterstock; 71, nito/Shutterstock; 74, boonlert saikrajang/Shutterstock; 76, hydra viridis/Shutterstock; 78, OPhotoSunnyDays/Shutterstock; 79, bbernard/Shutterstock; 82, wavebreakmedia/Shutterstock; 83, insta_photo/Shutterstock; 85, everst/Shutterstock